CONNECTING
555 Meaningful Questions for Friends to Build Lasting Relationships

CONNECTING

555 Meaningful Questions for Friends to Build Lasting Relationships

Deepen Friendships, Enhance Emotional Intelligence, and Navigate Life's Challenges with Questions for Friends

Aria Capri Publishing Group
Mauricio Vasquez

Toronto, Canada

Authors:

Aria Capri Publishing

Mauricio Vasquez

First Printing: December 2024

ISBN 978-1-998402-82-3 (Paperback)
ISBN 978-1-998402-83-0 (Hardcover)
ISBN 978-1-998402-84-7 (Ebook)

TABLE OF CONTENTS

Introduction: The Case for Deepening Friendships

Asking questions is, has been, and always will be at the heart of meaningful friendships. Questions open the door to deeper understanding, strengthen emotional bonds, and uncover new possibilities for connection in powerful and enduring ways.

Why is asking thoughtful and intentional questions important for fostering friendships?

First and foremost, asking the right questions builds trust. When you engage in thought-provoking conversations with friends—whether about shared experiences, emotions, or values—you create a foundation for mutual growth. These questions disrupt surface-level interactions, invite vulnerability, and spark the kind of dialogue that leads to stronger, more fulfilling relationships.

Questions also serve as bridges. They connect you to your friends' hearts and minds, showing that you value their stories, perspectives, and feelings. When you ask meaningful questions—and truly listen to the answers—you foster understanding, resolve conflicts, and create a space where authenticity thrives.

But here's the truth: not all questions are created equal. In friendships, it's easy to fall into routines, relying on casual or superficial questions that don't fully explore the depth of your connection. Worse yet, avoiding difficult conversations or failing to act on what you learn can create distance and tension. Asking the right questions—insightful, open-ended, and intentional—goes beyond simply "catching up." It's about strengthening your bonds and cultivating the resilience needed to navigate life's complexities together.

Imagine this: what if misunderstandings between you and a friend are rooted in unspoken expectations? What if your connection could grow exponentially by exploring shared goals or addressing unresolved conflicts? Without asking the right questions, you may miss opportunities to deepen your friendship, heal emotional wounds, or celebrate the unique strengths each person brings to the relationship.

The poet Rainer Maria Rilke once said, "Live the questions now." This wisdom resonates deeply when it comes to building meaningful friendships. A thoughtful question asked at the right moment can open a path to understanding, renew trust, and inspire mutual growth.

You don't need to spend endless hours figuring out which questions to ask. I've done that for you.

This book offers 555 thoughtfully crafted questions designed to strengthen connections, enhance emotional intelligence, and provide practical tools for navigating the challenges of friendships. These questions are tailored for anyone seeking to nurture deeper bonds, from lifelong companions to new acquaintances.

With these questions as your guide, you'll unlock the power of curiosity, promote intentionality in your friendships, and build a foundation for relationships that endure. Whether you're aiming to foster mutual growth, resolve lingering conflicts, or simply celebrate the joy of friendship, this book provides the tools you need to grow closer with the people who matter most.

Your journey to more meaningful friendships starts here. Let's get curious together.

Guidelines for Asking Powerful Questions to Deepen Friendships

Friendships thrive on curiosity, trust, and shared understanding. Thoughtful questions encourage deeper connections, foster empathy, and navigate challenges with kindness. This section offers guidelines to craft meaningful conversations that strengthen bonds, inspire collaboration, and create lasting, fulfilling relationships.

1. Effective questions are open or focused, depending on the context
   Friendship-building questions invite discovery. Open-ended questions spark curiosity and genuine connection because they can't be answered with a simple "yes" or "no." These questions encourage thoughtful conversations, allowing friends to explore feelings, values, and shared experiences in meaningful ways.

2. Effective questions strengthen understanding and mutual respect
   To nurture friendships, your questions should invite honesty, challenge assumptions, and encourage empathy. Thoughtful questions help friends focus on key aspects of their relationship—whether it's resolving misunderstandings, celebrating milestones, or simply enjoying each other's company.

3. Effective questions prioritize shared growth over personal agendas
   Friendships flourish when questions are asked to support and inspire both individuals rather than serve one person's interests. The goal is to create a safe space where both friends feel heard and valued, avoiding attempts to steer the conversation toward predetermined outcomes.

4. Effective questions encourage emotional connection
   Deep bonds often emerge from shared feelings and perspectives. By inviting a personal response—how a friend feels about a situation or what they value

most—you can foster trust and intimacy. Emotionally engaging questions help friends connect on a deeper, more authentic level.

5. Effective questions shift focus from problems to possibilities

   When friendships face challenges, thoughtful questions can redirect attention from tensions to opportunities for growth. These questions help friends envision how they can move forward together, deepening their connection rather than dwelling on conflicts or misunderstandings.

6. Effective questions inspire exploration, not defensiveness

   To maintain an open and trusting atmosphere, frame questions with curiosity and kindness. Avoid phrasing that might feel accusatory or judgmental. Instead, use language like "What do you think?" or "How might we work through this?" to encourage constructive and compassionate dialogue.

7. Effective questions promote collaboration over control

   The most impactful friendship-building questions empower both parties to contribute ideas and solutions, fostering a sense of shared responsibility. Collaboration strengthens friendships, allowing both individuals to feel ownership of their relationship's growth and direction.

8. Effective questions offer flexibility and personalization

   The questions in this book are designed to adapt to the unique dynamics of your friendships. Each question includes two pre-determined terms relevant to the topic, providing inspiration and structure. Additionally, a blank space invites you to personalize the question, making it more meaningful to your specific situation. This format ensures the questions feel both guided and uniquely yours.

9. Less is more when asking friendship-building questions
Simple, clear questions often lead to the most profound conversations. Overly complicated or multi-layered questions can overwhelm or confuse. A concise question like, "What do you value most about our friendship?" or "What's one thing we could improve together?" can spark deep insights and heartfelt exchanges.

By following these guidelines, you can craft powerful questions that foster understanding, strengthen emotional bonds, and create lasting connections. Remember, the art of asking is as important as the conversations it inspires. Each question in this book serves as both a guide and an invitation to explore, deepen, and celebrate the friendships that bring joy and meaning to your life.

Tips for the Use of this Book

These tips are designed to help you get the most out of this book's 555 friendship-building questions. By adapting, combining, and expanding on these prompts, you can nurture deeper connections, foster mutual understanding, and create lasting, meaningful relationships.

- The chapters are guides, not rules: The questions are grouped into chapters based on themes like trust, emotional growth, and conflict resolution. While these chapters provide structure, many questions are versatile and can inspire connection across different friendship dynamics.
- Start with curiosity and active listening: Strong friendships begin with understanding. Pay close attention to your friend's feelings, stories, and perspectives. Consider the emotions, patterns, and values in your friendship to guide how you use these questions most effectively.
- Tailor questions to your unique friendships: For the best results, adapt the questions to fit your relationships. Whether navigating a close bond, strengthening a casual friendship, or building a new connection, a well-tailored question can spark transformative conversations.
- Combine and build for deeper connection: Friendships thrive on layered understanding. Feel free to combine questions or ask follow-ups to explore emotions, uncover shared values, and deepen mutual trust. This layered approach can lead to surprising and meaningful insights.
- Each question offers options for flexibility: Many questions include two pre-determined terms or concepts to inspire your thinking, along with a blank space to personalize the question. This structure encourages both creativity and relevance, making the questions adaptable to your unique situations.

- Follow-up questions foster growth: One question often leads to another. Don't be afraid to dig deeper with follow-up questions to clarify understanding, navigate challenging emotions, or explore shared aspirations. Follow-ups can unlock new perspectives and deepen bonds.
- Make the questions your own: While the questions in this book are crafted for clarity and inspiration, feel free to adjust the language to suit your tone, personality, or the dynamics of your friendships. Personalizing the questions can make them even more impactful.
- Keep it simple and intentional: Friendships flourish with thoughtful communication. Ask one question at a time, keeping your focus clear and purposeful. This approach allows for deeper reflection and authentic responses that strengthen your connection.

By using these tips as a guide, you'll not only create more meaningful conversations but also build a foundation of trust, resilience, and mutual growth in your friendships. Remember, each question in this book is an invitation to strengthen your connections and celebrate the joy of human connection. Let curiosity and intentionality lead the way!

Dear Valued Reader

Thank you for choosing this book as your guide to deepening connections and fostering meaningful friendships. Your decision to embark on this journey toward greater emotional intelligence and stronger relationships means the world to me.

As an independent author, I rely on the feedback and support of readers like you to help this book reach others who are eager to enhance their friendships and build lasting, fulfilling bonds. Your insights not only inspire me but also encourage others to explore how thoughtful questions can transform their relationships.

If this book has resonated with you, I kindly ask for your support by leaving a review. Your feedback helps spread the word to readers who, like you, value the importance of curiosity, intentionality, and thoughtful communication in cultivating meaningful friendships.

To share your thoughts, simply scan the QR code below, which will take you directly to the review section on the e-commerce platform where you purchased this book. Your time and kindness will make a significant impact,  and I truly appreciate your effort in helping this message reach more readers.

Thank you for your trust, support, and commitment to making your friendships more resilient and rewarding.

Regards,

Mauricio

Empower Your Connections:
Discover More Tools to Strengthen Relationships.
Scan the QR Code Today

Chapter 1. Emotive Overdependence

Friendships thrive on mutual support, but relying too much on a friend for emotional fulfillment can strain even the strongest bonds. This chapter invites you to reflect on emotional dynamics, balance your needs with those of others, and foster healthier, more resilient relationships. Use these questions to cultivate self-awareness, open dialogue, and a shared understanding, ensuring friendships grow through trust and reciprocity.

1. What actions can you take to balance your (emotional needs/self-reliance/_____) in your friendships this week?

2. How do you define healthy (support/boundaries/_____) in a friendship, and how can you communicate this?

3. What steps could you take to strengthen (mutual respect/shared space/_____) in your relationships?

4. How can you ensure (reciprocity/independence/_____) in the emotional dynamics of your friendships?

5. What (emotions/patterns/) do you notice when you rely on your friend for (comfort/advice/)?

6. How can you manage (expectations/emotional load/_____) when your friend is unavailable for support?

7. What small actions can help you foster (emotional independence/self-confidence/_____) without compromising your friendships?

8. How can you recognize when your (needs/boundaries/_____) are placing strain on a friend's emotional capacity?

9. What (habits/assumptions/) could you adjust to encourage more balanced (communication/support/) in your friendships?

10. How can you better communicate your (needs/concerns/) while respecting your friend's (emotional boundaries/time/)?

11. In what ways could you share your (gratitude/appreciation/_____) for your friend's emotional support?

12. How can you distinguish between (helpful support/emotional dependence/_____) in your friendships?

13. What does (trust/self-awareness/_____) mean to you when it comes to balancing emotional dynamics in a friendship?

14. How can you support your own (emotional growth/self-soothing/_____) without solely relying on a friend?

15. What strategies can you use to avoid (overburdening/exceeding/_____) your friend's capacity for emotional support?

16. How can you work together to create (mutual understanding/emotional space/_____) in your friendship?

17. What (external resources/personal practices/) could you explore to reduce reliance on a friend for (validation/comfort/)?

18. What are some indicators that (emotional reciprocity/healthy boundaries/_____) are thriving in your friendships?

19. How can you address feelings of (insecurity/loneliness/_____) without overburdening your friend?

20. What (tools/skills/) could help you nurture your (self-reliance/resilience/) in emotionally challenging situations?

21. How do you respond when a friend sets (boundaries/limitations/_____), and how can you adjust your expectations?

22. What's one way you could shift your (mindset/approach/) to prevent overdependence on a friend for (guidance/encouragement/)?

23. How can you practice (gratitude/self-compassion/_____) to cultivate a healthier balance of emotional reliance in your friendships?

Chapter 2. Fear of Rejection

Fear of rejection can hold us back from fully opening up in friendships, yet vulnerability is essential for building trust and deeper connections. This chapter invites you to reflect on your fears, reframe them, and cultivate courage in expressing your authentic self. These questions are designed to foster openness, reduce hesitation, and strengthen bonds through mutual understanding and acceptance.

1. What steps can you take to explore (vulnerability/trust/_____) in your friendships without fear of rejection?

2. How can you reframe your (insecurities/expectations/_____) about opening up to your friends?

3. What (assumptions/stories/) are you telling yourself about how your friend perceives your (feelings/actions/)?

4. How do you think addressing your (hesitations/concerns/_____) with your friend could transform your connection?

5. What (qualities/traits/) do you value most about your friend that make you feel (safe/understood/)?

6. How can you express your (feelings/thoughts/_____) without fear of being judged or misunderstood?

7. What small actions could you take to test the waters of (openness/authenticity/_____) with a trusted friend?

8. How do you distinguish between your (fears/perceptions/) and your friend's (actual behavior/intentions/)?

9. What (shared experiences/positive moments/_____) can you reflect on to build confidence in your friend's acceptance of you?

10. How can you communicate your (needs/worries/) to your friend in a way that fosters (understanding/empathy/)?

11. What does (acceptance/rejection/_____) mean to you, and how does it shape the way you show up in your friendships?

12. How can you work through your fear of (misunderstanding/rejection/_____) to nurture stronger bonds with your friend?

13. What strategies can help you focus on (positive outcomes/authentic connections/_____) rather than potential rejection?

14. What role does (self-compassion/self-acceptance/_____) play in overcoming your fear of opening up to friends?

15. What's one (conversation/topic/_____) you've avoided due to fear, and how can you approach it differently?

16. How can you invite your friend to share their (thoughts/feelings/_____) to create a more reciprocal sense of openness?

17. What's the worst outcome you fear from sharing your (truth/vulnerability/_____), and how likely is it to happen?

18. How could sharing your (insecurities/experiences/_____) strengthen trust and intimacy in your friendship?

19. How can you distinguish between being (authentic/transparent/_____) and oversharing in your relationships?

20. What can you do to build your (confidence/resilience/_____) in the face of potential rejection?

21. How can you turn your fear of rejection into an opportunity for (growth/connection/_____) with your friends?

22. What (past experiences/beliefs/_____) contribute to your hesitation, and how can you reframe them?

23. How do you want your friend to perceive your (vulnerability/courage/_____), and how can you communicate this?

Chapter 3. Unresolved Conflicts

Unresolved conflicts can silently strain even the strongest friendships. This chapter provides thought-provoking questions to help you address past disagreements, understand lingering tensions, and foster resolution. By encouraging honest communication and empathy, these prompts empower friends to rebuild trust and strengthen their bond.

1. What steps can you take to address (misunderstandings/hurt feelings/_____) in your friendship this week?

2. How can you create a safe space to discuss (past disagreements/unspoken concerns/_____) with your friend?

3. What (perspectives/assumptions/_____) might you reconsider to better understand your friend's side of the conflict?

4. How has this (disagreement/silence/) affected the (trust/connection/) in your friendship?

5. What actions can you take to ensure (forgiveness/empathy/_____) becomes part of resolving your conflicts?

6. What might help you and your friend reflect on the (causes/consequences/_____) of your disagreement?

7. How can you approach discussing (sensitive topics/old arguments/_____) without triggering defensiveness?

8. What (shared goals/common values/_____) can guide your efforts to resolve lingering issues?

9. How can you express your (regret/understanding/_____) to begin mending any hurt caused by the conflict?

10. What have you learned about (yourself/your friend/_____) from this unresolved issue?

11. What's one (habit/pattern/_____) you could change to prevent similar conflicts in the future?

12. How can you balance being (honest/respectful/_____) when addressing unresolved tensions with your friend?

13. What (questions/conversations/_____) might help uncover the root cause of your disagreement?

14. How can you ensure that (apologies/accountability/_____) are genuine and meaningful during reconciliation?

15. What would an ideal resolution to this (conflict/misunderstanding/_____) look like for both of you?

16. How can you communicate your (intentions/hopes/_____) for resolving the issue with your friend?

17. What (words/actions/_____) might help rebuild trust after a period of tension?

18. How can you use this conflict as an opportunity to (grow/strengthen/_____) your friendship?

19. What can you both do to ensure the (issue/mistake/_____) doesn't resurface in the future?

20. How can you show (patience/respect/_____) if your friend needs more time to process the conflict?

21. What role does (pride/ego/_____) play in keeping the issue unresolved, and how can you address this?

22. What are you willing to let go of (resentment/expectations/_____) to move forward together?

23. How might resolving this (tension/conflict/) enhance the (quality/meaning/) of your friendship?

Chapter 4. Jealousy and Envy

Jealousy and envy can silently erode trust and mutual respect in friendships. This chapter helps you explore these feelings, fostering deeper understanding and encouraging gratitude, self-awareness, and positive communication. Use these questions to transform envy into growth and appreciation, strengthening your connections.

1. What steps can you take to turn feelings of (envy/self-doubt/_____) into opportunities for personal growth?

2. How can you express gratitude for your friend's (achievements/qualities/_____) while celebrating your own?

3. What (triggers/situations/_____) make you feel jealous, and how can you address them constructively?

4. How might your friend's (successes/relationships/_____) inspire you to pursue your own goals?

5. What assumptions are you making about your friend's (intentions/feelings/_____) that may not be true?

6. How can you communicate your (insecurities/feelings/_____) without letting jealousy damage your connection?

7. What's one way you could celebrate your friend's (accomplishments/opportunities/_____) to reinforce trust?

8. How can you focus on (self-appreciation/self-growth/_____) instead of comparing yourself to your friend?

9. What (qualities/values/_____) do you admire most about your friend, and how can you acknowledge them?

10. How might jealousy be an indicator of your (desires/ambitions/_____), and how can you act on these?

11. What shared (goals/values/_____) could you both focus on to strengthen your friendship during challenging times?

12. How can you use open dialogue to address (jealousy/envy/_____) before it creates a wedge between you?

13. What role does (comparison/expectation/_____) play in your feelings, and how can you shift your perspective?

14. How can you remind yourself of your unique (strengths/achievements/_____) to combat feelings of inadequacy?

15. What (emotions/needs/_____) might your jealousy reveal, and how can you explore them constructively?

16. How can you ensure your feelings of (envy/frustration/_____) do not overshadow the value of your friendship?

17. What's one small step you can take to build your own (confidence/success/_____) rather than focusing on comparisons?

18. How might you approach a conversation about (boundaries/expectations/_____) to reduce envy in your friendship?

19. What actions could help you and your friend foster (mutual encouragement/shared goals/_____) during moments of tension?

20. How can you reframe jealousy as an opportunity to deepen your (understanding/self-awareness/_____)?

21. What's one way you can practice (self-compassion/gratitude/_____) to reduce feelings of envy?

22. How might your friend's (strengths/relationships/_____) complement your own journey, rather than compete with it?

23. What steps could you take to celebrate both your (unique path/shared experiences/_____) and your friend's successes?

Chapter 5. Emotional Maturity Disparities

Emotional maturity impacts how we navigate misunderstandings and meet each other's emotional needs in friendships. This chapter explores the dynamics of differing emotional capacities, offering questions to foster empathy, bridge gaps, and cultivate stronger, more balanced connections through understanding and intentional growth.

1. What steps can you take to better understand your friend's (emotional capacity/reactions/_____) in challenging situations?

2. How can you express your (feelings/expectations/_____) in a way that respects your friend's emotional readiness?

3. What (tools/strategies/_____) could help you navigate moments of emotional misunderstanding with your friend?

4. How can you encourage (patience/empathy/_____) when handling differences in how you and your friend process emotions?

5. What role do (vulnerability/communication/_____) play in bridging gaps in emotional maturity?

6. How can you approach conversations about (needs/boundaries/_____) to reduce tension caused by emotional differences?

7. What (habits/beliefs/_____) might you reconsider to create more emotional balance in your friendship?

8. How can you support your friend's (growth/understanding/_____) without overstepping or overwhelming them?

9. What small actions can you take to nurture (trust/emotional openness/_____) when differences arise?

10. How can you gently address your friend's (responses/defenses/_____) when emotions run high?

11. What (qualities/values/_____) can you focus on to appreciate your friend's emotional style?

12. How can you better express your need for (support/understanding/_____) without creating conflict?

13. What's one way you could practice (self-awareness/empathy/_____) in moments of emotional tension?

14. How can you use (shared experiences/mutual goals/_____) to strengthen your bond despite emotional differences?

15. What triggers your own (reactions/frustrations/_____) in emotionally charged situations, and how can you manage them?

16. How can you invite your friend to share their (feelings/needs/_____) without pressuring them?

17. What (expectations/boundaries/_____) could you adjust to create more harmony in your friendship?

18. How can you respond to your friend's (emotional withdrawal/overexpression/_____) with compassion?

19. What does (growth/emotional balance/_____) look like in a friendship with differing emotional capacities?

20. How can you turn emotional misunderstandings into opportunities for (connection/personal growth/_____)?

21. What (conversations/actions/_____) can help you both navigate emotional challenges more effectively?

22. How can you ensure your own (emotional needs/self-care/_____) are met without overburdening your friend?

23. What's one way you can celebrate your friend's (progress/efforts/_____) in developing emotional awareness?

Chapter 6. Unspoken Expectations in Love

Unspoken expectations often linger beneath the surface in relationships, shaping emotions, behaviors, and outcomes. This chapter invites you to uncover, express, and align these hidden desires. Through thoughtful dialogue, these questions will help you foster understanding, deepen intimacy, and build healthier, more fulfilling connections rooted in mutual clarity and respect.

1. What unspoken (needs/assumptions/_____) do you think might be influencing your relationship dynamics, and how can you address them?

2. How can you and your partner establish a shared understanding of (boundaries/priorities/_____) to prevent misaligned expectations?

3. What (habits/patterns/_____) in your relationship might indicate unexpressed desires or unmet needs?

4. In what ways do you rely on (nonverbal cues/indirect communication/_____) to express your expectations, and how could this be improved?

5. What steps can you take to clarify your (goals/preferences/_____) in the relationship with your partner?

6. How might unspoken (beliefs/fears/_____) about love be impacting your ability to communicate openly?

7. What (assumptions/expectations/_____) about affection do you hold, and how can you share them with your partner?

8. What strategies could help you and your partner align your (future plans/day-to-day routines/_____) more effectively?

9. What role do (cultural influences/personal experiences/_____) play in shaping your unspoken expectations?

10. How might clarifying your (intentions/values/_____) strengthen your connection with your partner?

11. What unspoken (sacrifices/compromises/_____) have you made in the relationship, and how can you express these constructively?

12. How do you address unmet (needs/desires/_____) in a way that fosters growth and avoids resentment?

13. What (language/approach/_____) best helps you and your partner articulate hidden expectations?

14. What (rituals/routines/_____) could help create a space to regularly discuss your expectations?

15. How do you approach resolving differences in (perspectives/priorities/_____) when they aren't initially voiced?

16. What unspoken (rules/standards/_____) might you be holding your partner to, and are they aware of them?

17. How could you reframe your (expectations/limitations/_____) to be more inclusive of your partner's individuality?

18. What role does (vulnerability/trust/_____) play in creating an environment for open communication?

19. How can you differentiate between (assumptions/realities/_____) when interpreting your partner's actions or words?

20. What practices might help uncover unspoken (desires/fears/_____) before they escalate into conflict?

21. What (tools/conversations/_____) could help you and your partner better articulate your shared vision for the relationship?

22. How do you and your partner manage (disappointments/misunderstandings/_____) when unspoken expectations arise?

23. What (milestones/shifts/_____) in your relationship might require a reevaluation of previously unspoken expectations?

Chapter 7. Lack of Empathy

Empathy is the bridge that connects hearts in friendships. When missing, it can create feelings of neglect and misunderstanding. This chapter offers questions to explore, nurture, and rebuild empathy in friendships, fostering mutual respect, connection, and emotional support.

1. How can you express your (needs/perspective/_____) to a friend without feeling misunderstood or dismissed?

2. What steps can you take to better understand a friend's (emotions/challenges/_____) when they seem distant?

3. What (signals/cues/_____) might you be missing that indicate a lack of empathy in your friendship?

4. How could you approach a friend about feeling (undervalued/disconnected/_____) in a way that fosters understanding?

5. What role does (active listening/emotional validation/_____) play in creating a more balanced friendship?

6. What practices could help you and your friend explore each other's (needs/limitations/_____) more empathetically?

7. What strategies could improve how you show empathy for your friend's (experiences/perspectives/_____)?

8. How do you identify when your (assumptions/biases/_____) might be limiting your ability to empathize?

9. What unspoken (fears/expectations/_____) might be contributing to a perceived lack of empathy in your friendship?

10. How could you and your friend set clearer (boundaries/expectations/_____) to encourage more mutual understanding?

11. What tools might help you recognize when a friend needs (support/space/_____) rather than advice?

12. How can you initiate a conversation about improving (emotional awareness/mutual respect/_____) in your friendship?

13. What (memories/actions/_____) can you reflect on that demonstrate empathy in your friendship's history?

14. How can you balance your (needs/desires/_____) while still showing empathy for your friend's experiences?

15. What would demonstrating (patience/understanding/_____) in a moment of tension look like for you?

16. What aspects of your (communication style/emotional expression/_____) might hinder empathy in your friendships?

17. What steps can you take to foster (trust/vulnerability/_____) when empathy feels one-sided?

18. How do you respond when your friend dismisses your (feelings/concerns/_____), and how could empathy play a role?

19. What role do shared (values/experiences/_____) play in nurturing empathy in your friendship?

20. How can you turn feelings of (resentment/disappointment/_____) into an opportunity to grow empathy in your friendship?

21. What (questions/approaches/_____) could you use to better understand a friend's silence or emotional withdrawal?

22. How can you differentiate between a lack of (awareness/capacity/_____) for empathy versus a lack of care?

23. What practices might help you and your friend develop a habit of (checking in/clarifying feelings/_____) more regularly?

Chapter 8. Low Self-Esteem

Low self-esteem can influence the way friends perceive themselves and their worth within a relationship, creating barriers to trust and connection. This chapter offers thoughtful questions to support, uplift, and nurture confidence, fostering deeper trust and mutual respect.

1. What steps can you take to affirm your friend's (strengths/value/_____) in a way that feels authentic to them?

2. How do you create an environment that encourages (trust/vulnerability/_____) in your friendship?

3. What (habits/beliefs/_____) might your friend hold that hinder their ability to feel secure in the friendship?

4. How can you approach conversations about (insecurities/needs/_____) without making your friend feel judged?

5. What role does (self-awareness/empathy/_____) play in supporting a friend with low self-esteem?

6. What specific (actions/words/_____) have you noticed help your friend feel more appreciated?

7. How can you gently challenge your friend's (negative self-talk/unrealistic expectations/_____) to promote healthier self-esteem?

8. What practices can you introduce to celebrate your friend's (progress/accomplishments/_____) together?

9. What (questions/approaches/_____) might help your friend share their insecurities more openly?

10. do you balance offering (support/encouragement/_____) with respecting your friend's independence?

11. What (boundaries/communication strategies/_____) can help ensure your friend doesn't feel overly dependent in the friendship?

12. What are ways you can model (confidence/self-compassion/_____) to inspire your friend?

13. How do you respond when your friend dismisses their own (achievements/qualities/_____), and how could you shift that dynamic?

14. What (positive reinforcements/encouraging routines/_____) could help you both reinforce self-worth in your friendship?

15. How can you use moments of (gratitude/humor/_____) to gently uplift your friend when they feel down about themselves?

16. What role do (mutual understanding/shared goals/_____) play in building confidence in your friendship?

17. How can you identify when your friend's (withdrawal/defensiveness/_____) is a result of low self-esteem?

18. What specific (experiences/activities/_____) could help your friend feel more valued and included?

19. What steps can you take to reframe your friend's (doubts/self-perceptions/_____) without minimizing their feelings?

20. How do you ensure your (feedback/support/_____) is constructive rather than unintentionally critical?

21. What (tools/techniques/_____) could you use to encourage your friend to embrace their individuality?

22. How can you use your friend's (interests/strengths/_____) to foster a more positive self-view?

23. What (stories/experiences/_____) from your friendship can you revisit to remind your friend of their importance to you?

Chapter 9. Differing Attachment Styles

Attachment styles—secure, anxious, or avoidant—shape how we connect and respond to others. This chapter explores how mismatched styles influence friendships, offering thoughtful questions to bridge gaps, nurture understanding, and align behaviors for deeper, more harmonious connections.

1. How do your (reactions/expectations/_____) in friendships reflect your attachment style, and how might they impact your friend?

2. What strategies could help you navigate differences in (communication styles/emotional needs/_____) with your friend?

3. How can you use (curiosity/empathy/_____) to better understand your friend's attachment style?

4. What (boundaries/practices/_____) can you set to honor both your needs and your friend's attachment preferences?

5. How can you recognize when your (attachment patterns/assumptions/_____) are creating tension in the friendship?

6. What role do (trust/security/_____) play in helping your friend feel more comfortable in the relationship?

7. What (signals/cues/_____) might indicate your friend's attachment style, and how can you respond thoughtfully?

8. How do you approach discussing (intimacy/connection/_____) with a friend whose attachment style differs from yours?

9. What steps can you take to balance your (independence/closeness/_____) in a way that feels fair to both of you?

10. How can you reframe your friend's (avoidance/anxiety/_____) as an opportunity for growth in your friendship?

11. What (actions/conversations/_____) have you noticed help create security in your friendship?

12. How might your friend's (past experiences/personal growth/_____) influence their attachment behaviors, and how can you support them?

13. What role do (patience/open-mindedness/_____) play in bridging attachment differences between you and your friend?

14. What (challenges/opportunities/_____) arise from your attachment styles, and how can you address them together?

15. How can you initiate a conversation about (expectations/vulnerability/_____) without overwhelming your friend?

16. What shared (activities/goals/_____) could help foster a sense of security in your friendship?

17. How do you navigate moments when your friend's (behavior/response/_____) feels inconsistent with your expectations?

18. What tools could help you better understand and adapt to your friend's (triggers/preferences/_____) in the relationship?

19. How can you use (compassion/validation/_____) to reassure a friend with an anxious attachment style?

20. What strategies could help you respect a friend's need for (space/autonomy/_____) while staying connected?

21. How do you address your own (insecurities/patterns/_____) that may contribute to attachment challenges in the friendship?

22. What (rituals/practices/_____) can help build trust and consistency in a friendship with differing attachment styles?

23. How can you celebrate your friend's (efforts/progress/_____) in navigating attachment challenges, and what can you learn from them?

Chapter 10. Unspoken Expectations

Unspoken expectations can silently strain even the strongest friendships. This chapter helps identify and address hidden needs, fostering open communication and mutual clarity. These questions encourage honest dialogue to reduce frustration and nurture stronger, more understanding relationships.

1. What steps can you take to communicate your (needs/priorities/_____) more clearly in your friendship?

2. How do you handle situations where your (expectations/assumptions/_____) haven't been met, and what can you learn from them?

3. What role do (honesty/clarity/_____) play in helping your friend understand your needs?

4. How can you use (examples/conversations/_____) to express your expectations without creating pressure?

5. What specific (requests/actions/_____) would help your friend feel more confident in meeting your needs?

6. How might your (assumptions/preferences/_____) be unintentionally creating tension in your friendship?

7. What are some unspoken (rules/expectations/_____) you've noticed in your friendship, and how do they affect you?

8. How can you balance expressing your (desires/limits/_____) while respecting your friend's perspective?

9. What (words/gestures/_____) can you use to clarify your needs without feeling vulnerable?

10. What role do (past experiences/personal values/_____) play in shaping your unspoken expectations?

11. How might you encourage your friend to share their (concerns/expectations/_____) more openly?

12. What (tools/conversations/_____) could help uncover hidden assumptions in your friendship?

13. How can you approach moments where your (needs/expectations/_____) feel ignored with understanding rather than frustration?

14. What steps can you take to transform your (assumptions/frustrations/_____) into opportunities for connection?

15. How can you reframe unmet (needs/expectations/_____) as opportunities to grow communication in your friendship?

16. What role does (patience/self-reflection/_____) play in addressing unspoken assumptions with your friend?

17. How might setting clearer (boundaries/practices/_____) improve the balance in your friendship?

18. What (habits/phrases/_____) could you introduce to make sharing expectations feel more natural?

19. What unspoken (needs/hopes/_____) could you share with your friend to foster greater mutual understanding?

20. How can you invite your friend to clarify their (needs/preferences/_____) in a way that feels supportive?

21. What (signals/actions/_____) from your friend might you have misinterpreted due to your own expectations?

22. How can you better navigate moments when your (assumptions/desires/_____) don't align with reality?

23. What practices could help you both regularly discuss your (intentions/expectations/_____) to prevent misunderstandings?

Chapter 11. Grief or Loss

Grief and loss can create deep emotional shifts that test friendships, especially when both individuals are coping with shared pain. This chapter offers thoughtful questions to support healing, foster understanding, and strengthen bonds during times of sorrow and transition.

1. How can you support each other's (healing/emotions/_____) while honoring your individual grieving processes?

2. What role do (shared memories/mutual support/_____) play in helping you navigate loss together?

3. How can you express your (needs/boundaries/_____) during moments when grief feels overwhelming?

4. What specific (actions/gestures/_____) can help you show compassion for each other in this time of loss?

5. How do you both define (healing/resilience/_____), and how might those definitions guide your connection?

6. What (traditions/routines/_____) could help honor the memory of what was lost while maintaining your friendship?

7. How can you create space for (silence/vulnerability/_____) without placing pressure on each other to perform healing?

8. What (assumptions/expectations/_____) about grief could you address to prevent misunderstandings in your friendship?

9. How might your differing approaches to (emotions/coping/_____) be an opportunity for mutual growth?

10. What (phrases/support systems/_____) have you found helpful or unhelpful in moments of grief?

11. How can you support your friend when their (grieving pace/emotional needs/_____) differ from your own?

12. What role do (shared stories/joint experiences/_____) play in keeping your connection alive amidst loss?

13. How can you use your (creativity/presence/_____) to offer comfort without assuming what your friend needs?

14. What specific (values/qualities/_____) in your friendship can provide strength during this difficult time?

15. How do you balance your own (emotions/pain/_____) while being present for your friend?

16. What role does (reflection/humor/_____) play in helping both of you process grief together?

17. How can you approach moments of (distance/tension/_____) that arise from different grieving styles?

18. What (activities/conversations/_____) might help you both feel connected while honoring your individual healing paths?

19. How can you ensure that your (shared memories/support/_____) deepen your connection rather than strain it?

20. What practices could help you recognize when your friend might need (space/empathy/_____) rather than advice?

21. What (lessons/perspectives/_____) have you both gained from this shared experience of grief?

22. How can you acknowledge the (impact/importance/_____) of your loss while also focusing on your friendship?

23. What are some ways you can celebrate your (growth/resilience/_____) together as you navigate this difficult time?

Chapter 12. Group Dynamics

Navigating friendships within a group can bring unique challenges, from managing alliances to addressing jealousy or favoritism. This chapter helps you explore group dynamics with curiosity and care, fostering inclusivity, understanding, and stronger relationships among all members.

1. How can you promote (fairness/inclusivity/_____) when navigating group decisions or activities?

2. What role do (communication/clarity/_____) play in addressing misunderstandings within your group?

3. How do you balance (one-on-one connections/shared experiences/_____) to maintain harmony in the group?

4. What (signs/patterns/_____) of favoritism might exist in the group, and how can they be addressed?

5. How do you approach resolving (jealousy/tensions/_____) without creating further conflict?

6. What (values/boundaries/_____) can your group establish to create a more supportive environment?

7. How can you encourage (empathy/respect/_____) when someone feels excluded within the group?

8. What strategies can you use to address (alliances/misunderstandings/_____) that might disrupt group cohesion?

9. How do you manage feelings of (jealousy/insecurity/_____) when someone in the group receives more attention?

10. What (rituals/practices/_____) can the group adopt to ensure everyone feels valued and included?

11. How can you ensure your (individual needs/group priorities/_____) align in the context of your friendships?

12. What (situations/dynamics/_____) in the group bring out the best in everyone, and how can you nurture them?

13. How do you navigate conversations about (favoritism/exclusion/_____) without making others defensive?

14. What role does (active listening/open feedback/_____) play in resolving group disagreements?

15. How can you celebrate (individual achievements/group milestones/_____) without causing friction among members?

16. What steps can you take to include quieter or less involved (friends/perspectives/_____) in group discussions?

17. How can you balance addressing (group harmony/individual concerns/_____) when conflicts arise?

18. What (positive habits/communication techniques/_____) could improve the group's ability to navigate differences?

19. How do you express your (preferences/concerns/_____) without seeming divisive in a group setting?

20. What role do (assumptions/expectations/_____) play in group dynamics, and how can they be challenged?

21. What strategies can you use to address (imbalanced roles/unequal effort/_____) within the group?

22. How do you encourage (authenticity/support/_____) while maintaining a sense of unity in your friendships?

23. What (shared values/common goals/_____) can you all focus on to strengthen the group's connection?

Chapter 13. Cultural or Social Norms

Friendships often bridge diverse cultural backgrounds and social norms, which can lead to rich connections or unintentional misunderstandings. This chapter explores ways to navigate and celebrate these differences through thoughtful questions that foster empathy, respect, and deeper understanding.

1. How can you approach your friend's (traditions/values/_____) with curiosity and respect?

2. What steps can you take to better understand your friend's (background/perspective/_____) and how it influences their behavior?

3. How do you navigate differences in (communication styles/social customs/_____) to maintain harmony in your friendship?

4. What (assumptions/stereotypes/_____) might you hold about your friend's culture, and how can you challenge them?

5. How can you create space for conversations about (cultural differences/unspoken norms/_____) without discomfort or judgment?

6. What role do (empathy/patience/_____) play in resolving misunderstandings rooted in cultural or social norms?

7. What (shared experiences/common values/_____) can you focus on to bridge cultural differences in your friendship?

8. How do you express your (needs/boundaries/_____) in a way that aligns with your friend's social expectations?

9. What strategies can you use to address (misinterpretations/differing expectations/_____) caused by cultural nuances?

10. What (rituals/practices/_____) from your friend's culture could you learn from or incorporate into your life?

11. How do you respond when your friend's (norms/preferences/_____) differ from your own in social settings?

12. What (questions/actions/_____) can you take to show genuine interest in your friend's cultural identity?

13. How can you balance honoring your own (background/beliefs/_____) while respecting your friend's cultural differences?

14. What role do (language/expressions/_____) play in shaping your understanding of each other's experiences?

15. What (behaviors/expectations/_____) might unintentionally cause friction in your cross-cultural friendship?

16. How can you celebrate your friend's (heritage/customs/_____) in ways that feel authentic and meaningful?

17. What role do (traditions/shared celebrations/_____) play in strengthening your understanding of each other?

18. How might your friend's (upbringing/community norms/_____) influence how they view certain aspects of your friendship?

19. What (challenges/opportunities/_____) arise from blending your social norms, and how can you address them together?

20. What strategies could help you and your friend navigate differing (celebrations/lifestyles/_____) with mutual respect?

21. What (resources/conversations/_____) could help deepen your understanding of your friend's cultural identity?

22. How can you turn moments of (misunderstanding/disagreement/_____) into opportunities to learn more about each other?

23. What (stories/shared experiences/_____) from your friendship reflect how you've grown through cultural differences?

Chapter 14. Power Imbalances

Power imbalances in friendships can create challenges such as dependency or resentment when one person holds more influence or control. This chapter offers thought-provoking questions to explore, understand, and rebalance dynamics for healthier, more equitable relationships.

1. How do you recognize when your (actions/decisions/_____) might contribute to a power imbalance in your friendship?

2. What steps can you take to ensure your (opinions/preferences/_____) don't overshadow your friend's voice?

3. How do you feel about the (roles/dynamics/_____) in your friendship, and what changes might improve balance?

4. What (boundaries/practices/_____) can help address feelings of dependency or resentment in your friendship?

5. How do you navigate situations where one friend's (needs/priorities/_____) dominate decisions in the relationship?

6. What (assumptions/expectations/_____) about your friend's role might unintentionally create an imbalance?

7. How can you encourage (equal participation/shared decision-making/_____) in your friendship dynamics?

8. What (behaviors/habits/_____) might unintentionally reinforce unequal power dynamics, and how can they be shifted?

9. How do you approach conversations about (fairness/respect/_____) when you feel the power dynamic is uneven?

10. What role do (trust/mutual understanding/_____) play in maintaining balance in your friendship?

11. How can you express your (needs/concerns/_____) in a way that feels empowering to both you and your friend?

12. What (specific actions/adjustments/_____) could help redistribute responsibility or influence in your friendship?

13. How might your friend's (confidence/personality/_____) affect how power dynamics are perceived or felt?

14. What steps can you take to avoid creating (dependency/control/_____) in your interactions?

15. How can you support your friend in asserting their (preferences/needs/_____) more effectively?

16. What (behaviors/words/_____) from your friend make you feel empowered, and how can you reciprocate?

17. What role does (feedback/self-awareness/_____) play in addressing imbalances in your friendship?

18. How can you balance your (dominance/assertiveness/_____) with creating space for your friend's contributions?

19. What (values/agreements/_____) could help both of you establish a more equitable friendship?

20. How do you handle situations where one of you feels (overlooked/overburdened/_____) in the relationship?

21. What practices could help you both reflect on and adjust your (roles/expectations/_____) over time?

22. What (tools/conversations/_____) could help address and repair any feelings of resentment caused by imbalances?

23. How can you celebrate each other's (strengths/individuality/_____) while maintaining a sense of equality in your friendship?

Chapter 15. Misaligned Social Circles

Integrating friends and family into a friendship can be challenging when social circles differ. This chapter explores ways to bridge gaps, foster mutual acceptance, and navigate the complexities of blending relationships for stronger, more inclusive connections.

1. How can you introduce your (friends/family/_____) in a way that makes them feel comfortable and welcomed?

2. What steps can you take to understand your friend's (social dynamics/group preferences/_____) better?

3. How can you navigate differences between your (friend group/social traditions/_____) without creating tension?

4. What (activities/conversations/_____) could help bridge the gap between your social circles?

5. How do you balance your (loyalty/commitments/_____) to different groups while maintaining your friendship?

6. What role does (openness/empathy/_____) play in integrating each other's friends or family?

7. What strategies can you use to address (discomfort/resistance/_____) from your social circle about your friend?

8. How might your (preferences/norms/_____) affect your ability to connect with your friend's social group?

9. What practices can help you both feel (included/valued/_____) in each other's social settings?

10. How do you handle situations where your (friends/family/_____) may not understand your connection with your friend?

11. What (shared values/common goals/_____) could you highlight to help align your social circles?

12. What (boundaries/preferences/_____) should you both establish to prevent conflicts between your groups?

13. How can you ensure your (friendship/dynamics/_____) remain strong even if your social circles don't overlap?

14. What steps could you take to navigate (jealousy/competition/_____) between your friend and your social group?

15. What (assumptions/stereotypes/_____) about your friend's social circle might you need to challenge?

16. How can you support your friend if they feel (excluded/overwhelmed/_____) by your social group?

17. What (shared experiences/joint activities/_____) could help blend your social circles in a positive way?

18. What role do (mutual respect/flexibility/_____) play in creating harmony between your groups?

19. How can you approach conversations about (discomfort/misunderstandings/_____) with your friend regarding your social circles?

20. What (insights/perspectives/_____) have you gained from interacting with your friend's social circle?

21. What (traditions/rituals/_____) could you introduce to make interactions between your groups more enjoyable?

22. How can you celebrate your (differences/similarities/_____) while still honoring your unique social groups?

23. What steps could help you both navigate (expectations/potential conflicts/_____) related to integrating your social circles?

Chapter 16. Gossip and Rumors

Misunderstandings and hurt feelings. This chapter provides thought-provoking questions to help address breaches of trust, clarify intentions, and rebuild connection through honest communication and accountability.

1. How can you address (misinformation/breaches of trust/_____) in a way that strengthens your friendship?

2. What steps can you take to clarify your (intentions/feelings/_____) if a rumor has caused tension?

3. How do you approach a friend who has shared (private information/misinformation/_____) without your consent?

4. What role does (forgiveness/accountability/_____) play in repairing trust after gossip?

5. How can you ensure your (reactions/feedback/_____) don't escalate a situation involving rumors?

6. What practices could help you and your friend build (transparency/mutual respect/_____) moving forward?

7. What (assumptions/feelings/_____) might you need to address if a rumor about you is spreading?

8. How do you decide when to confront (rumors/gossip/_____) versus letting them go?

9. What (boundaries/conversations/_____) could you establish to prevent gossip from disrupting your friendship?

10. How can you support a friend who feels (betrayed/vulnerable/_____) due to gossip?

11. What steps can you take to model (trustworthiness/integrity/_____) in your friendships?

12. What role does (clarity/compassion/_____) play when addressing a friend involved in spreading rumors?

13. How can you distinguish between (constructive feedback/negative gossip/_____) when discussing others?

14. What (questions/actions/_____) could help you understand a friend's motivations for gossiping?

15. How might your own (words/behaviors/_____) contribute to an atmosphere of trust or gossip?

16. What (values/agreements/_____) could help both of you prioritize loyalty over gossip in your friendship?

17. How can you address feelings of (embarrassment/hurt/_____) if you've been the subject of a rumor?

18. What (support/insight/_____) could you offer a friend who unintentionally caused harm through gossip?

19. What practices could help both of you redirect (negative conversations/unhealthy patterns/_____) in your friendship?

20. What role does (honesty/self-reflection/_____) play in resolving misunderstandings caused by rumors?

21. How do you ensure your responses to (rumors/misinformation/_____) align with your personal values?

22. What (actions/words/_____) can rebuild trust if you've unintentionally participated in gossip?

23. How can you use moments of (miscommunication/vulnerability/_____) to strengthen rather than weaken your bond?

Chapter 17. Comparisons with Other Friends

Comparing friendships to others can create unnecessary dissatisfaction or pressure, straining relationships. This chapter encourages self-reflection and open dialogue to celebrate the uniqueness of each friendship, helping readers cultivate gratitude, acceptance, and deeper emotional connection with their friends.

1. How can you shift your focus from (comparison/appreciation/_____) to better celebrate your unique friendship?

2. What (qualities/values/_____) do you cherish in your friendship that make it distinct from others?

3. How do you recognize when (expectations/assumptions/_____) are being influenced by comparisons with other friendships?

4. What role does (gratitude/self-awareness/_____) play in valuing your relationship without comparisons?

5. How can you use (reflection/conversation/_____) to address feelings of dissatisfaction caused by comparisons?

6. What (needs/boundaries/_____) might you need to clarify to avoid pressure in your friendship?

7. How can you balance observing other friendships without (envy/discontent/_____) affecting your own?

8. What (shared experiences/common interests/_____) make your friendship unique and fulfilling?

9. How do you approach moments when you feel (insecure/disconnected/_____) about your friendship?

10. What steps can you take to strengthen your (confidence/communication/_____) in your relationship?

11. What (expectations/social norms/_____) might be shaping how you compare your friendship to others?

12. How can you express your (appreciation/needs/_____) without creating pressure on your friend?

13. What (misunderstandings/assumptions/_____) might arise from comparing your friendship to others?

14. How do you celebrate your friend's (unique qualities/personal growth/_____) instead of comparing them to others?

15. What role does (trust/vulnerability/_____) play in creating a stronger bond between you and your friend?

16. What (practices/mindsets/_____) could help you embrace your friendship as it is, without comparisons?

17. How do you navigate feelings of (jealousy/inadequacy/_____) when seeing other friendships?

18. What (strengths/opportunities/_____) can you identify in your friendship that other relationships may not have?

19. How can you use (challenges/differences/_____) as opportunities for growth rather than comparison?

20. What role does (social media/peer influence/_____) play in how you view your friendships?

21. How can you communicate your (insecurities/hopes/_____) to your friend without creating distance?

22. What (positive qualities/shared moments/_____) can you focus on to appreciate your friendship more fully?

23. How might comparing less and celebrating more improve your (bond/understanding/_____) with your friend?

Chapter 18. Boundaries in Professional Friendships

Blending professional and personal relationships can enrich connections but also create challenges. This chapter explores how to maintain mutual respect, clear boundaries, and effective communication to navigate professional friendships while fostering trust, collaboration, and meaningful personal connections.

1. How can you clarify your (expectations/boundaries/_____) to maintain professionalism while deepening your friendship?

2. What role do (trust/respect/_____) play in ensuring a healthy balance between work and personal interactions?

3. How can you navigate moments when (work pressures/personal feelings/_____) affect your friendship?

4. What strategies could help you address (misunderstandings/conflicts/_____) that arise from overlapping roles?

5. How do you ensure your (friendship/professionalism/_____) remains unaffected by workplace challenges?

6. What (practices/conversations/_____) can help separate work-related discussions from personal interactions?

7. How might your (actions/words/_____) unintentionally blur professional boundaries in your friendship?

8. What steps can you take to express (discomfort/concerns/_____) without straining your friendship?

9. How do you handle situations where (work dynamics/power imbalances/_____) impact your personal connection?

10. What (values/shared goals/_____) can guide your decisions in maintaining professionalism in your friendship?

11. How can you offer (support/feedback/_____) in a way that respects both personal and professional boundaries?

12. What (boundaries/agreements/_____) can you establish to protect both your friendship and your workplace roles?

13. How do you address feelings of (jealousy/competition/_____) that may arise in professional settings?

14. What (qualities/habits/_____) do you most appreciate in your friend as both a colleague and a confidant?

15. How can you balance being (honest/objective/_____) when providing professional feedback to a friend?

16. What (conversations/actions/_____) could help strengthen your friendship without compromising workplace dynamics?

17. How do you recognize when your (personal involvement/work commitments/_____) may need to be rebalanced?

18. What role do (open communication/mutual understanding/_____) play in preserving the integrity of your friendship?

19. How can you navigate (criticism/praise/_____) in the workplace without affecting your personal connection?

20. What practices could ensure that your (friendship/professionalism/_____) supports rather than hinders your career growth?

21. How do you set clear (limits/expectations/_____) to ensure fairness and respect in professional interactions?

22. What (shared experiences/common goals/_____) help you maintain a meaningful friendship alongside professional collaboration?

23. How can you celebrate your (successes/bond/_____) in ways that honor both your personal and professional connection?

Chapter 19. Impact of Social Media

Social media has transformed how we connect, but it can also create misunderstandings or tension through oversharing, lack of engagement, or misinterpretations. This chapter explores ways to navigate these challenges, fostering meaningful connections both online and offline.

1. How can you balance your (online presence/privacy/_____) to maintain harmony in your friendship?

2. What role do (likes/comments/_____) play in how you perceive your friend's engagement with you online?

3. How do you address feelings of (neglect/misinterpretation/_____) caused by social media interactions?

4. What (boundaries/practices/_____) could help you both feel respected when it comes to online sharing?

5. How can you use (transparency/communication/_____) to prevent misunderstandings related to social media?

6. What (assumptions/expectations/_____) about online interaction might be creating tension in your friendship?

7. How can you ensure your (posts/interactions/_____) reflect your values and respect your friend's preferences?

8. What (steps/conversations/_____) could help you address oversharing or privacy concerns in your friendship?

9. How do you feel about your friend's (posting habits/online activity/_____), and how might this affect your connection?

10. What strategies could help you navigate (unintentional exclusions/social media conflicts/_____) without harming your friendship?

11. How can you express your (concerns/appreciation/_____) about your friend's online engagement in a constructive way?

12. What (tools/perspectives/_____) could help you distinguish between online actions and real-life intentions?

13. How do you approach situations where (tags/posts/_____) make you feel uncomfortable or excluded?

14. What role does (honesty/empathy/_____) play in resolving social media misunderstandings in your friendship?

15. How can you both ensure your (digital communication/boundaries/_____) align with your offline relationship?

16. What (values/priorities/_____) guide how you and your friend interact on social platforms?

17. How might your friend's (online persona/preferences/_____) differ from their offline self, and how do you navigate that?

18. What (steps/actions/_____) could you take to avoid comparing your friendship to others on social media?

19. How can you use (shared interests/mutual goals/_____) to make your social media interactions more meaningful?

20. What (practices/conversations/_____) could help address feelings of jealousy or exclusion sparked by online activity?

21. How do you interpret your friend's (response times/interaction patterns/_____) without overanalyzing their meaning?

22. What role does (digital detox/quality time/_____) play in strengthening your friendship outside of social media?

23. How can you celebrate your (friendship/memories/_____) in a way that feels authentic online and offline?

Chapter 20. Exclusion and FOMO (Fear of Missing Out)

Feeling excluded or experiencing FOMO can create a sense of neglect in friendships. This chapter invites thoughtful reflection on addressing these emotions, fostering openness, and building stronger connections through understanding, inclusion, and intentional communication.

1. How can you express your (feelings/concerns/_____) about being left out in a way that fosters understanding?

2. What (steps/actions/_____) can you take to ensure you feel included without placing pressure on your friends?

3. How do you interpret your friend's (intentions/behavior/_____) when you feel excluded from an event or conversation?

4. What role does (self-reflection/communication/_____) play in addressing feelings of FOMO in your friendships?

5. How can you approach conversations about (inclusion/boundaries/_____) to strengthen your bond?

6. What (activities/conversations/_____) could help you feel more connected to your friend's life?

7. How do you balance respecting your friend's (autonomy/privacy/_____) with your need for inclusion?

8. What (assumptions/expectations/_____) might you need to let go of to reduce feelings of FOMO?

9. How can you communicate your (desire to be included/preferences/_____) without feeling vulnerable?

10. What role do (social norms/personal insecurities/_____) play in how you perceive exclusion?

11. How do you navigate moments when your (availability/choices/_____) lead to missing out with friends?

12. What practices can help you reframe feelings of (neglect/disappointment/_____) into opportunities for growth?

13. How can you build trust with your friend to openly discuss (FOMO/exclusion/_____) without fear of judgment?

14. What (qualities/values/_____) in your friendship remind you of its importance despite occasional exclusions?

15. What (tools/strategies/_____) can you use to manage feelings of missing out on social events?

16. How can you celebrate your friend's (choices/connections/_____) while addressing your own feelings of exclusion?

17. What steps can you take to ensure your (presence/efforts/_____) are recognized and valued in the friendship?

18. How can you encourage your friend to share (details/invitations/_____) in a way that feels inclusive?

19. What role do (honesty/empathy/_____) play in addressing misunderstandings around inclusion?

20. How can you use feelings of (isolation/FOMO/_____) to inspire deeper, more meaningful interactions?

21. What (activities/routines/_____) could help you stay connected with your friend when you're apart?

22. How can you reframe moments of (exclusion/FOMO/_____) to focus on your own well-being and priorities?

23. What role do (shared experiences/open dialogue/_____) play in ensuring both of you feel valued in the friendship?

Chapter 21. Social Expectations of Reciprocity

Reciprocity is a cornerstone of strong friendships, but imbalanced efforts in initiating plans or offering support can strain relationships. This chapter offers thoughtful questions to explore and realign mutual effort, fostering understanding, balance, and shared responsibility.

1. How can you balance your (efforts/expectations/_____) in initiating plans to ensure fairness in your friendship?

2. What role do (gratitude/open communication/_____) play in addressing imbalances in effort or support?

3. How do you feel when you're consistently the one to (initiate/contact/_____), and how can you address it constructively?

4. What (actions/gestures/_____) from your friend make you feel valued and supported?

5. How can you express your (needs/frustrations/_____) about imbalances without causing tension?

6. What (practices/conversations/_____) could help clarify your friend's willingness to reciprocate effort in the relationship?

7. How might your (assumptions/expectations/_____) about reciprocity impact your feelings toward your friend?

8. What (tools/approaches/_____) could help you address resentment if you feel unsupported?

9. How can you show appreciation for your friend's (efforts/support/_____), even if they differ from your expectations?

10. What (boundaries/agreements/_____) could help maintain balance in initiating plans or offering help?

11. How do you recognize when your (friendship dynamics/personal efforts/_____) are becoming one-sided?

12. What steps can you take to encourage (shared responsibilities/reciprocity/_____) in your friendship?

13. How can you ensure your (requests/expectations/_____) don't feel like obligations to your friend?

14. What role does (self-awareness/patience/_____) play in addressing perceived imbalances in effort or support?

15. How can you identify your friend's (limitations/preferences/_____) when it comes to giving and receiving support?

16. What (activities/rituals/_____) could help both of you contribute equally to your shared experiences?

17. How can you express your appreciation for your friend's (unique contributions/emotional support/_____) without focusing on perceived deficits?

18. What strategies can you use to discuss (imbalances/resentment/_____) in a way that strengthens your bond?

19. How do you navigate feelings of (guilt/frustration/_____) when reciprocity doesn't align with your expectations?

20. What (examples/conversations/_____) could help you recognize areas where you might need to give more?

21. How do you ensure that your (offers/help/_____) are not creating unspoken expectations for your friend?

22. What role do (shared values/common goals/_____) play in maintaining balance and reciprocity in your friendship?

23. How can you use moments of (imbalance/disconnection/_____) to reflect on and improve your relationship dynamics?

Chapter 22. Life Transitions

Life transitions—such as moving, changing jobs, marriage, or having children—can shift the dynamics and availability in friendships. This chapter offers reflective questions to help friends navigate these changes, maintain meaningful bonds, and adapt to evolving circumstances with empathy and care.

1. How can you show (understanding/support/_____) for your friend's life transition while maintaining your connection?

2. What role does (adaptability/communication/_____) play in helping your friendship thrive during major changes?

3. How do you feel when your friend's (availability/priorities/_____) shift, and how can you address it constructively?

4. What steps can you take to maintain (consistency/closeness/_____) when life transitions create distance?

5. How can you express your (needs/boundaries/_____) without placing pressure on your friend during a transition?

6. What (activities/traditions/_____) could help sustain your friendship as your circumstances evolve?

7. How might your friend's (choices/new responsibilities/_____) affect your perspective on your friendship?

8. What (emotions/expectations/_____) might you need to process when your friend experiences a major life change?

9. How do you support your friend when their (priorities/schedule/_____) limit their ability to spend time together?

10. What (shared goals/conversations/_____) can help you both adapt to changes in your friendship dynamics?

11. How can you celebrate your friend's (milestones/new opportunities/_____) without feeling left behind?

12. What role do (patience/understanding/_____) play in maintaining balance during a time of transition?

13. What (adjustments/boundaries/_____) could help ensure your friendship remains meaningful despite life changes?

14. How can you navigate feelings of (loss/disconnection/_____) if a life transition changes your friendship dynamic?

15. What (qualities/strengths/_____) in your friendship can help you both weather periods of change?

16. What steps can you take to stay (engaged/involved/_____) in your friend's life, even from a distance?

17. How do you ensure your (support/advice/_____) aligns with what your friend actually needs during their transition?

18. What role do (shared experiences/flexibility/_____) play in adapting to changes in each other's lives?

19. How might your friend's (new responsibilities/major decisions/_____) influence the way you connect?

20. What (actions/rituals/_____) could help maintain intimacy in your friendship despite shifting circumstances?

21. How do you approach conversations about (expectations/resentments/_____) that may arise during life transitions?

22. What (challenges/opportunities/_____) have these changes brought to your friendship, and how can you address them?

23. How can you use your friend's transition as an opportunity to strengthen your (communication/empathy/_____) and bond?

Chapter 23. Distance and Communication Gaps

Physical distance or infrequent communication can test the strength of friendships, creating feelings of disconnection over time. This chapter offers reflective and actionable questions to help bridge these gaps, nurture bonds, and maintain meaningful connections despite challenges.

1. How can you use (technology/shared activities/_____) to maintain a sense of closeness despite physical distance?

2. What role does (regularity/spontaneity/_____) play in keeping your communication alive and meaningful?

3. How do you feel when your friend is (unavailable/distant/_____), and how can you express this constructively?

4. What specific (habits/tools/_____) could you introduce to stay in touch more consistently?

5. How can you celebrate your friend's (milestones/daily life/_____) from afar in a way that feels personal?

6. What (traditions/check-ins/_____) could help you both stay connected despite a busy schedule?

7. How do you address feelings of (neglect/disconnection/_____) without placing blame on your friend?

8. What (methods/topics/_____) make your communication feel most meaningful when you catch up?

9. How do you balance your (efforts/expectations/_____) when physical distance affects your friendship?

10. What role do (empathy/patience/_____) play in navigating periods of infrequent communication?

11. What steps can you take to ensure your (messages/conversations/_____) are engaging and uplifting?

12. How do you interpret your friend's (response times/interaction patterns/_____), and how does this affect your feelings?

13. What (creative approaches/shared projects/_____) could make staying in touch more enjoyable for both of you?

14. How do you prioritize your (friendship/time/_____) when life gets busy for both of you?

15. What role do (shared goals/mutual understanding/_____) play in maintaining your bond across distances?

16. What (questions/updates/_____) can you share to make your conversations more personal and engaging?

17. How can you address moments when your (expectations/needs/_____) for communication aren't met?

18. What practices could help you both feel (valued/included/_____) in each other's lives despite the distance?

19. How do you handle situations where (time zones/schedules/_____) make it difficult to connect?

20. What (traditions/rituals/_____) could you establish to look forward to regular check-ins or reunions?

21. How can you show appreciation for your friend's (efforts/presence/_____) even when communication is limited?

22. What role does (reflection/gratitude/_____) play in strengthening your connection when you feel distant?

23. How might your friend's (circumstances/communication style/_____) shape your approach to staying connected?

Chapter 24. Different Priorities

Life's varied demands—work, family, hobbies, and other pursuits—can sometimes create misalignment in friendships, leading to disconnects in availability or shared interests. This chapter offers questions to bridge these gaps and nurture understanding, balance, and mutual respect.

1. How can you respect your friend's (commitments/choices/_____) while expressing your need for connection?

2. What role do (honesty/patience/_____) play in navigating differing priorities in your friendship?

3. How can you find common ground despite differing (schedules/interests/_____)?

4. What (activities/rituals/_____) could you both commit to in order to stay connected?

5. How do you approach conversations about (disappointment/expectations/_____) when priorities seem misaligned?

6. What (shared goals/values/_____) help keep your friendship strong despite differing focuses?

7. How can you ensure your (friendship/time together/_____) feels meaningful even when availability is limited?

8. What (steps/actions/_____) could you take to understand your friend's current priorities better?

9. How do you address feelings of (neglect/disconnection/_____) caused by differing commitments?

10. What role do (communication/empathy/_____) play in adjusting your expectations for each other?

11. How might your friend's (workload/family needs/_____) shape their availability, and how can you adapt?

12. What (boundaries/agreements/_____) can you establish to maintain a balance in your friendship?

13. How can you celebrate your friend's (achievements/interests/_____) without feeling disconnected from their life?

14. What (creative ideas/shared activities/_____) could help you stay involved in each other's lives?

15. How do you communicate your (concerns/feelings/_____) about the time you spend together without placing blame?

16. What (tools/conversations/_____) could help you both manage expectations around availability and priorities?

17. How can you show appreciation for your friend's (efforts/presence/_____) even during busy periods?

18. What (adjustments/mindsets/_____) could help you embrace the changes in your friendship dynamics?

19. How might you use (mutual understanding/perspective-taking/_____) to support each other's different paths?

20. What (questions/connections/_____) can help you explore new ways to align your interests and priorities?

21. How do you navigate situations where (shared plans/existing routines/_____) are disrupted by life's demands?

22. What role does (flexibility/compassion/_____) play in keeping your friendship thriving despite differing commitments?

23. How can you both prioritize (check-ins/moments of connection/_____) to maintain closeness?

Chapter 25. Economic or Financial Disparities

Financial differences between friends can create discomfort, jealousy, or challenges in planning shared activities. This chapter provides thought-provoking questions to foster understanding, mutual respect, and creative approaches for maintaining strong connections despite differing financial situations.

1. How can you acknowledge and respect your friend's (financial boundaries/preferences/_____) without making assumptions?

2. What (activities/gestures/_____) can help you both enjoy quality time together without financial stress?

3. How do you approach conversations about (splitting costs/planning activities/_____) in a way that feels fair?

4. What role does (transparency/communication/_____) play in navigating financial differences in your friendship?

5. How can you celebrate your friend's (success/choices/_____) without feeling uncomfortable or jealous?

6. What (values/shared interests/_____) can guide your decisions when planning affordable activities together?

7. How do you balance your (expectations/plans/_____) when your financial situations differ?

8. What strategies can you use to avoid creating (pressure/discomfort/_____) for your friend during outings?

9. How do you address feelings of (insecurity/envy/_____) about financial differences in your friendship?

10. What (tools/conversations/_____) could help you both feel included in planning activities that suit everyone's budget?

11. How might your friend's (spending habits/priorities/_____) shape your shared experiences, and how do you adapt?

12. What role do (gratitude/perspective/_____) play in maintaining a positive dynamic despite financial disparities?

13. What (boundaries/agreements/_____) could help prevent financial differences from impacting your connection?

14. How can you express your (preferences/limitations/_____) about spending without feeling embarrassed?

15. What (creative ideas/shared goals/_____) can make your friendship richer without relying on financial resources?

16. How can you encourage conversations about (money/expenditures/_____) without creating tension or awkwardness?

17. What role does (honesty/empathy/_____) play in ensuring both of you feel valued regardless of income?

18. How can you reframe financial differences as opportunities to explore (new activities/fresh perspectives/_____) together?

19. What (practices/rituals/_____) could you both adopt to minimize the impact of economic disparities in your plans?

20. How do you handle moments when (jealousy/misunderstanding/_____) arise due to differences in financial circumstances?

21. What (actions/adjustments/_____) could help you and your friend create more equitable experiences?

22. How can you express gratitude for your friend's (generosity/support/_____) without feeling indebted or uncomfortable?

23. What (lessons/opportunities/_____) have you gained from navigating financial differences in your friendship?

Chapter 26. Health Challenges

Health challenges—whether physical, mental, or caregiving-related—can impact the balance of support and understanding within a friendship. This chapter explores ways to nurture resilience, empathy, and open communication, strengthening friendships through life's toughest moments.

1. How can you offer (empathy/understanding/_____) to your friend during their health challenges without overstepping boundaries?

2. What role do (patience/communication/_____) play in maintaining your connection during periods of imbalance?

3. How can you express your (concern/support/_____) without making your friend feel overwhelmed or judged?

4. What (actions/words/_____) from your friend help you feel appreciated when supporting them through health struggles?

5. How can you balance your own (needs/emotions/_____) while being there for a friend dealing with chronic illness or caregiving?

6. What (habits/rituals/_____) could help you both maintain a sense of normalcy in your friendship despite health challenges?

7. How do you navigate conversations about (sensitive topics/limitations/_____) in a way that feels safe for both of you?

8. What (practices/resources/_____) can help you better understand your friend's mental or physical health journey?

9. How might your friend's (energy levels/emotional state/_____) shape how you interact with them?

10. What (questions/actions/_____) could help you check in on your friend without feeling intrusive?

11. How can you acknowledge your friend's (resilience/vulnerability/_____) without minimizing their experiences?

12. What steps can you take to offer (practical help/emotional support/_____) without overstepping boundaries?

13. What (values/shared goals/_____) guide how you both navigate health-related changes in your friendship?

14. How do you handle moments when (misunderstandings/expectations/_____) arise due to health-related challenges?

15. What role does (honesty/self-awareness/_____) play in maintaining balance in your friendship during tough times?

16. How can you celebrate your friend's (progress/strengths/_____) without placing undue expectations on their recovery or caregiving?

17. What (tools/conversations/_____) could help you both communicate your needs more clearly during health struggles?

18. How do you show (gratitude/compassion/_____) when your friend opens up about their challenges?

19. What (activities/traditions/_____) could help sustain your friendship despite the limitations of health issues?

20. How can you encourage your friend to seek (support/self-care/_____) while respecting their autonomy?

21. What role do (boundaries/shared understanding/_____) play in preventing burnout in your friendship?

22. What steps can you take to process your own (emotions/concerns/_____) when supporting a friend with health challenges?

23. How can you use moments of (vulnerability/growth/_____) to deepen your connection and mutual support?

Share Your Wisdom

Thank you for joining me on this journey to deepen connections and build more meaningful friendships. I hope this book's questions have inspired reflection, sparked heartfelt conversations, and provided valuable tools to nurture lasting and fulfilling relationships.

Now, I invite you to share your wisdom with others. By sharing your thoughts about this book, you can help inspire fellow readers to embrace curiosity, intentionality, and thoughtful communication in their friendships. Your feedback has the power to guide others toward building more resilient and joyful connections.

 To leave your review, please scan this QR code.

Your support means so much to me, and I'm truly grateful for your time and insights.

Thank you.

Mauricio